Introductio

Primary Schools are currently involving pupils in projects researching the 'Home Front in World War II'.

As a grandparent I was questioned and related my memories of that era when I was a child in Brechin. My combined interest in Local History prompted the writing of several articles which appeared in the Brechin Advertiser.

To meet numerous requests the articles have now been produced in a collective form, hopefully to be enjoyed by fellow Brechiners and others alike.

Mhairi Pyott

For the Brechiner

By

Mhairi Pyott

Invermark
Books

First published by InverMark Books in 2008

InverMark Books
20 Ladysmith Road
Cheltenham
GL52 5LQ

www.invermarkbooks.co.uk

Typeset by InverMark Books in 12 point Times New Roman

Printed and Bound by: Stoate & Bishop
                        Cheltenham

ISBN 13:   978-0-9554201-39

British Library Cataloguing in Publication Data:
A catalogue record for this book is available from The British Library

Cover design: Hebrideas

Photos and painting of Brechin Bridge by the author

Dedicated to my Mother,

Elizabeth Pyott Petrie

Chapters

1

Were They Good Days?

All the talk was about underwear parties and who had been elected as President of the Ladies Circle. The conversation of the young mothers had little to interest someone of my age group, waiting to escort my grandson safely home.

I stood gazing across the school wall into the empty playground. Soon it would be bursting with the shouts of pleasure as about one hundred five and six years old bairns rushed out to freedom.

Had things been the same when I attended the 'infants school' all those many years ago?

Miss Sherret had been my first teacher, when I was enrolled at the tender age of four years old, at Damacre Road School, Brechin.

Outbreak of War and the need of women to work in the munitions factories, prompted the government into early school placements.

No fancy computers then. How well I could remember the small brown case to carry my slate, skailie (slate pencil) and a small Oxo tin with a damp cloth to clean my slate.

Before that tearful first morning my mother had burned my name on the wooden frame around the slate with a red hot poker.

"You're a big lassie now, drink up your milk, do as the teacher tells you and you'll be fine. Remember if you hear the siren then run for the air raid shelter, after you have put on your gas mask. Mam will be here at home when you get out at four."

Perhaps there had been more said but basically that was the message given to me and my other classmates.

One girl in my class, I had recognised, as she lived with her Granny across the close from mine. Our playing together had

1

brought me rather a painful experience. That was after I had two beads surgically removed from my nose, at the Infirmary, with a pair of vicious looking forceps, by Miss Duke, of the V.A.D.

Granny had been none too happy when I announced before Grandad "We were just playing at being Grannies and taking snuff up our noses, like you do."

I can still recall the look that passed between them.

My mother, who was a very loving and caring person, perhaps influenced by the trouble I had caused smacked my backside as a warning of "what to expect should I not behave myself."

Miss Sherret never took such drastic actions. There must have been times when she was sorely tempted. Air raid shelter drill must have been a teacher's nightmare.

"Come along now, hurry up, quickly without running into the shelter, where we will be safe."

We all sat on the seats, a wooden sparred bench the length of the dark, dingy and damp smelling, windowless, narrow corridors, designed to promote our survival.

One of the teachers would hand out a sweet to each of us.

"Now put on your gas masks and we will have a sing song." What had Ten Green Bottles and Underneath the Spreading Chestnut Tree sounded like? The adjudicators at the Music Festivals would have had their work cut out reporting on our efforts.

Some of the class would start crying for their Mum's. They were mostly the evacuees. My special friend had come from York, where the bombing had been bad.

There had been whole trainloads of evacuees arriving at the station. They had marched to the Salvation Army Hall in Union Street. The labels tied to their collars, gas masks slung over their shoulders, brown parcels of clothes under their arms.

After tea and refreshments they were taken to their temporary homes to meet the unknowns, who had volunteered to care for them.

At four o'clock I would run along with the other children who lived in the street. We all had keys tied with ribbon or a string tied around our necks.

"The bairns need to get in the house if we are held up and late in getting home."

The mothers who worked part time finished at four o'clock to be home about the same time as we arrived. Some had to pick up the younger children from the newly built nursery. Even the babies in my young day had to do their bit for the War Effort, by being separated from their mothers who were saving Britain in the manufacture of bombs.

Free at last after tea. Out to play around the back doors.

'Shoppies' in the outside lavatory. Grown-ups did not approve of this game. With several families sharing the use of our 'shop', for it's legitimate purpose, we seldom found it free, for open business.

A concert in the washing house. What a grand stage the boiler made. "There's somebody's Mam shouting. Sing up louder and we'll say we never heard them," one of the older bairns would say. "Are you going to get saved at the Sallies tomorrow?" "I don't like going to the Juniors or the Young Soldiers." What a choice of activities!

"If you go forward and get saved, you get a slice of dumpling after." Yes I was saved.

"Would you bairns do as you are told and get away home before it's black dark," was the orders of the washing taker in, from the communal drying green.

"The Bobbies and the Air Raid Warden will get you if you don't get a move on."

We were so innocent and safe apart from the threat of Hitler's War.

"Oh there you are. I thought maybe you were lost in the dark. Run up to the chip shop for a penny bag for your supper. That's a good girl. Take the torch and remember to shine it on the ground because of the black out."

What a treat a poke of chips was. No fear of the dark and passing the end of dark closes. There was nothing to be frightened of but Hitler and all the Dad's were away from home to sort that out.

The chips were eaten on the way home. At first so hot you had to grip them between your teeth and blow. When you reached the bottom of the paper bag the last few were congealed in a soggy mass of salt, grease and vinegar. Fingers licked clean, before touching the polished brass door knob.

"You'll have to go out again with the Menages[1], the Bridge Street one Temperance Hall and Union Street ones. The bairn is sleeping and I can't manage myself. Run like the wind for it will soon be closed at eight o'clock. Tomorrow is Saturday and you'll get a long lie."

"What's happened to your skirt it's torn on the back?"

"Must have been that nail on the lavvie wall for hanging the paper squares."

"Need to try and mend it then for there's not enough clothing coupons or money to get another one. You can't go to the school with a hole in your skirt."

The school bell rang.

"They'll all be out in a minute." said the young girl who had joined me at the wall.

Sure enough out came a mad rush of blue, white and grey. Ties squint, shirt tails half tucked in waist bands. Blue blazers trailing from shoulders. School bags of all colours and decorations. Power Rangers, My Little Pony and Fireman Sam.

"Hi there Gran, this is the work I did on the computer this afternoon," said the joy of my heart, handing me a long sheet of print out paper.

Before I had time to answer he added. "Can you take the car around by Sam's house as I want him to come for tea and play in our garden?"

---

[1] A weekly savings club

The same type of arrangements were being made by the young mothers who had been waiting beside me.

"Yes if you can pick the girls up from Brownies, I'll see to the boys from football training. One of the men can pick up the older ones from Orchestra and Choir practice. It will be easy for them after they have been to the meeting at the High School about the 'Children and Drugs awareness' lecture."

No one from the concert in the washing house, but of course everybody has utility rooms now. No outside lavvies. No drugs awareness either. Granny's snuff was enough for us and even then we weren't brave enough to try the real thing. Hitler was our only bogey man. There never seemed to be 'funny men' to offer sweets and take us away forever.

Things had certainly changed since my young days at infant school. Had it been a change for the better, was technology giving our bairns a better chance in life?

I wonder!!

2

Run to the Soshie

Have you got your club card?" asked the girl at the supermarket check out.

"Yes it's somewhere. I've got it with me," I answered trying to retrieve what was left of my housekeeping allowance and plastic cards, from my young grandson, who was enjoying a fine rake through the contents of my purse.

I looked at the queue behind me, all grandparents like myself coping with little ones while their parents were at work.

"Here it is." I said trying to wrench it from my little darling's mouth.

The girl said nothing but glowered then wiped it with a duster produced from below the till, like a magician pulling a rabbit from a hat.

"You should look after your card for it means money to you a the end of the day." she scolded.

"Yes I'll do that in future. Sorry for the bother."

I began to think just how much money will I have saved with my club card. I was about to say. 'Bet I'll not save as much as you got from the Soshie Dividend, when I was a girl', when it registered just how young the till operator must be and probably had never heard of the Soshie, let alone the spending bonanza it generated twice yearly.

As I walked home laden with plastic carriers over the baby buggie, thankful that they were not cutting through my fingers, my thoughts returned to Soshie days. Message boys were there at the ready to deliver your groceries directly to your front door, or if you lived up the Latch or the posher districts, to the trades entrance.

They had specially equipped bicycles with huge baskets fitted to below the handle bars, above the front wheel. A large plate below the bar, between the seat and the handle bars, identified which shop was providing the delivery service, free of charge.

"Run up to the Soshie Office now that the checks are in and ask if they've been added up yet."

The Office, was in the middle of the High Street, beside the Ladies and Gents shoe shops. Soshie outlets of course.

When you finally got upstairs, to the inner sanctum, there was a high counter facing you.

"Yes can I help you?" came a distant voice from the far off side of the counter.

"Mam and Granny are wondering if the checks have been counted up yet?"

"What numbers are they?"

Those numbers were so vitally important. Whenever you purchased anything from a Brechin Co-operative Society shop and paid cash, you were given a hand written 'check' or receipt with the membership number and amount spent.

However, not only in Brechin, but as in all other co-operative shops, they worked the Black Book System. This was a credit system whereby the messages during the week supplied by the store were listed in the black book, kept by the member.

On Friday night, factory pay day, the book was balanced and cleared. With big families this could be a struggle from week to week. People were honest and although it sometimes required time to pay, always honoured their debts.

I was most familiar with the Southport Soshie. Jimmy Thomson was the man in charge. I cannot remember noticing, but it was said that Jimmy ran so fast around the shop that there were no corners, he had worn them all off in passing at speed to give the best possible service to his customers.

Sugar, Butter, Margarine, Lard, Cheese, Eggs and Biscuits. I still make up my shopping list in that order. It was only recently I appreciated why, when I was shown an old ration book. Rationing should have curbed grocery sales but we never seemed to want or go hungry. The co-operative shops were in every area of the city and not only were they food suppliers as already mentioned they also had shoe shops, the drapery, still operating at the top of the town, a tea room, later to become Cardo's, hardware department, beside the King's Picture house, the soshie hall above the Witchden butchers next to their dairy.

The Hall was the centre point for many a celebration and regularly in use for meetings of the Soshie Women's Guild and the Soshie Youth Club.

The Soshie Gala Day was eagerly looked forward to by all Brechin children. It didn't matter whether you attended Damacre or Andover School, you could march behind Dod Kean and the Silver Band up to the Public park, carrying your own cup for a drink. Every child was given a free bag which contained biscuits and buns and as many free drinks as they could manage. There was racing and sports events where competition was keen to collect the many prizes.

Of course there were other shops offering a choice of different items. They normally reaped most of the dividend pay out in November and May.

Mail order if it existed at that time, was unknown to me. There were of course salesmen from clothing firms outwith Brechin, who sold goods on deferred payments terms, or the never, never. These salesmen were often referred to as the travelling tailor or the flying draper. You could always tell the customers of one of those firms as they got off the Forfar bus, with their distinctive brown paper parcels tied with coarse string. The added cost of bus fares made this method of shopping less popular.

On reflection I suppose the Brechin Co-operative could supply everything needed from the cradle to the grave. There was also the added advantage of personal service.

Everyone in the shops knew the customers and the customers knew the staff.

All of these benefits and still a return of about half a crown in the pound off sales. That is equivalent of twelve and a half pence of today's money. I wonder if my club card and my local supermarket gives back as much as Brechin Co-operative Society did to it's members, when I was young?

3

New House

Glancing through the properties for sale in Brechin might be an indication of progress!

Such desirable homes with two public rooms, dining room, four bedrooms, two with en-suite. Double glazing, full central heating, double garage, garden front and rear. Never mind the price. This advert is not uncommon to todays readers. What sort of family would you expect to occupy such a modern home? Father, mother and two or maybe three children?

Pre World War II when Queens Park was built, to be allocated a flat there was just as sought after to the residents of the working class areas, Bridge Street, River Street, Montrose Street etc, as the desirable home in the property guide of today. They were wonderful homes after the cramped conditions of bringing up seven children in two rooms. To make matters worse there were many homes with no running water. Outside toilets to be shared with several other families 'on the land'. Water was carried in buckets normally from a communal tap outside the communal wash house. Each family by arrangement having their own day for the use of the laundry facilities and drying green. The boiler fire was lit at about six o'clock in the morning to allow for enough hot water to fill the large wooden tubs where the dirty wash was soaked, scrubbed against a rubbing board with a block of hard soap, then rinsed again in a tub full of clean water.

A wringer being a luxury most families could not afford, everything was wrung by hand. Washing and drying clothes for a family of nine, under those circumstances must have been a nightmare.

My grandparents could not believe their luck when they accepted the key to be the first occupants of a Queens Park three bedroomed flat, with living room, bathroom and kitchenette. What was more, it had hot and cold running water and electric lighting. It would be grand when the family not already left for homes of their own, returned from the armed services. It was all so bright and airy.

The electric light was so bright and glaring after the subdued lighting of a gas mantle. The kitchenette had a large white porcelain sink and a deep white porcelain washing tub, with a ribbed side for rubbing. No need for a board. Best of all there was in situ a gas boiler. Granny could wash all day, every day, to her hearts content because as an added bonus each flat had their own drying poles and it was exclusive to them. Yes there was a drawback. The flat was up three flights of stairs and to say that the gas boiler was temperamental was putting it mildly.

Granny, after trying unsuccessfully to stretch her arms from the control tap to the burner and throwing lighted matches at the escaping gas, decided to try other tactics. By this stage she had no eyebrows and the hair above where they had been was singed into a brown crop.

"Run to Nettie Thomson's shop and see if she's got wax tapers. They'll do the trick." Perhaps it worked that time I cannot remember. What I do know is that in the thirty odd years she lived in the house, the gas boiler could claim to have won most battles. On the losing days Granny reigned supreme by turning on the gas supply and poking a burning sheet of newspaper through the peephole to the burner. Others had difficulties with the hot water systems not working. No one had told them you had to light the living room fire to heat the back boiler. It sounds idiotic by today's standards but then people were not accustomed to such amenities.

There were fireplaces in the bedrooms. On a winters night it was wonderful to lie in bed cosy, with the twinkling glow of the red embers of the fire. What a wonderful end to the day. Next morning someone would have to carry all the ashes down to the bin, then hump all the buckets of coal up three flights of stairs for a warm evening by the fire. Coals were rationed, everything had to be saved to help the War Effort. The gas works sold 'gassy' cinders for sixpence a bag. After school and Saturday mornings would bring out all the old prams and carties. Down the Witchden into the queue the bags when filled were quite light to lift. No flames came from them but they gave off a tremendous heat when burning red. The bright electric light had to be dimmed. Shutters were put up on all the windows to block out even the smallest chink of light. Should the slightest pinpoint catch the eye of the Air Raid Warden there would be a banging on the door. "Get that light out or you'll get fined without any more warning."

At our home we did not have such modern wonders. It was gas lighting and outside toilet for us. And what a disaster if the gas mantle broke. This was often caused by the wind slamming a door shut, or folding the gas bracket back against the wall far enough to touch and damage the gauze.

McRitchie kept all the various sizes and styles of mantles. They were waxed for easy handling before attaching to the gas jet. The smell of 'burning off' the wax is unforgettable. Gas at this time was paid for by inserting pennies in a gas meter. Everyone was on the lookout for Fred Paterson, from the gas works, being in the street. If he was seen coming from the various closes near your home you knew that the meter was to be emptied of it's money . The amount of gas released by the insertion of a penny was always underestimated which resulted in most houses being given a rebate, all in pennies. What did that matter you could buy a lot of things with a pound of pennies when I was young.

Even a bundle of tapers for the gas boiler in Granny's new house.

4

The Pictures

Braveheart', 'Rob Roy' and similar film epics brought a revival of the Picture goers. I admit that I was one who had not seen a performance on the big screen since 'Close Encounters of the Third Kind'.

To be honest at the time my young daughter was not amused by my reaction to the then 'as near real space encounter of all time'. I fell asleep and was awakened by the quadraphonic sound system making the building, seats and myself vibrate as the screen portrayed the landing of an intergalactic vehicle.

The Scottish epics I enjoyed despite the blood, gore and poetic licence. My husband, most unusually for him, sat very quiet and white-faced while Mel Gibson acted his heart out.

"Are you disturbed by all the slashing off of arms and legs?" I asked while thinking he was not one to be squeamish or faint hearted at the sight of a good going barny.

"No I'm shell shocked at the arm and a leg it cost us to get into this place? We must have bought the seats the price I was charged." Even longer since he had an evening at the cinema! "One and nine pence, old money, for the dearest seats was what I last paid."

I suppose that could have been right.

The King's and the Regal Picture houses in Brechin charged the same entrance fee, something about ninepence, a shilling and one and ninepence, depending on the area where you were seated. Prices for the Saturday matinee were different.

Oh what a glorious occasion. You set off from home around one o'clock to join the queue for the Regal performance which started about two o'clock. By the time the box office opened, the queue could be down as far as the entrance to Cooper's lemonade factory. The cheap seats, several rows of wooden tip ups, were right down at the front, next to the screen. It was similar to lying with your head back for a dental inspection, to make it possible to view the action on the screen. Almost as painful when you tried to pull your chin down to your chest to stand erect for the playing of 'God Save the King' which ended all performances. The only time the seats and the auditorium vibrated was when the film broke down. Hundreds of pairs of feet stamped in unison to cries of "Get a penny in the meter." In times of emergency such as these the riot was very quickly quelled by Annie Asquith and Mrs Jack.

The beam of light from their torchlight flashing in your face, accompanied by the uttered threat "I'll see your mother and tell her how you behave." would have banished any enemies of William Wallace or Rob Roy. I cannot remember Mr Ritch, the theatre manager ever being at these afternoon performances.

In the evening he was there resplendent in evening dress, complete with bow tie.

Snow-White, Roy Rogers and of course Buck Rogers in Space, were all shown to the accompaniments of boos and cheers. 'Blossoms in the Dust' with the stars Greer Garson and Walter Pidgeon was my all time favourite. Poor little Tony crippled and wearing calipers, tenderly cared for by Greer and Walter. The happy ending climax, marked by tears, most probably due to pain and the need of a neck support after two hours of extended viewing. For weeks after we played out the heart rending scenes in our impromptu theatres, the wash-house or someone's half empty coal cellar.

'Song of Bernadette' was another all time favourite. As a special concession I was allowed to accompany Granny to the Kings to watch this spectacular production. There were two showings or houses Monday to Saturday. The first performance started about five forty five. With Dukie's and Smartie's not finishing until six o'clock at night from a six o'clock start in the morning, there was no great rush for the mid week early showing. Seated next to Granny in the dearer, downstairs velour covered tip up seats I felt like a royal princess. As an extra for being good I'd been given a bag of home made treacle toffee from Aggie Cross's shoppie in Union Street.

The moving tale of Bernadette Sabot and the appearance of the Virgin Mary kept Granny enthralled. Lourdes and all it's wonders to behold.

The toffee was a bit sickly and Granny took it for safe keeping putting it in the breast pocket of her jacket. As the film neared the end it was Granny who was fidgeting.

"Are you alright?" I asked concerned about her behaviour.

"Oh I'll be fine, watch the miracles and keep quiet."

Later I was to learn that she thought she was haemorrhaging and soaked with blood running onto her legs. Yes, it was only Aggie Cross's treacle toffee melting in the heat.

Some of the audience might have benefited from healing cures. The wounded soldiers in the audience were conspicuous with their bright blue uniforms and red ties. Allowed on pass from Stracathro Hospital, the walking wounded were a familiar sight about the town, but then so were so many other uniformed service men.

No uniformed usherettes or commissionaires for the Regal or the Kings, but they were grand places for entertainment when I was young.

5

Walking

When I drive past the walkers on the road at Kinnaird deer dykes I know I'm almost home for Brechin has always had associations with those who use their feet to enjoy what nature has on show. Sundays, our time off from being caring grandparents is when we indulge ourselves in what I consider to be my inherited hobby. How well I remember after the Sunday school at Maison Dieu being taken on various route marches by Grandad. "Shoulders back, chest forward and point your toes outwards." We must have looked like penguins as we took off to complete the various scenic tours that encircle our Ancient City.

Around the Stannochy, a short break was allowed in the middle of the Stannochy bridge to watch the eels squirming about in the muddy riverbed. Grandad would tell us of when he was a young man and had free time from working at the bleach-fields, he would join others fishing for fresh water oysters, to be rewarded with finding a much sought after Southesk Pearl. Past the little toll house that faced a triangular garden at the start of the Aberlemno Road. Along by Burghill farm. What a fascinating name. I believe it is said to be a derivation of 'Buttercup hill', however, like so many things in Brechin's past lost and forgotten with the passage of time. Similarly, no longer there, the 'Spring Well' half way up the hill.

What a welcome refreshing drink, from cupped hands, cool crystal clear water. According to the lesson to be learned at every rest stop, the origin of the spring was to be found in a crack between two rocks, in an abandoned quarry somewhere within the Hill Woods. The Reesk Quarry or similar sounding name sounds about right, but it was all so long ago! The other favourite watering place was on the journey by the cattle rake.

Brechin Bridge

Queens Park

Caledonian Railway Track

Brechin Caledonian Railway Station

East Mill Spinning Works

Maison Dieu Church

Fisherman near The Islandies

Painting of Brechin Bridge by the author

Up the loanie past Drumachlie farm, there were no houses then, just berryfields, on towards the cottar houses at Pitforthie. Strategically placed by the roadside was a bench type seat. We could never take time to sit down though, for we were eager to get a drink at the roadside pump in a little grassed recess off the road. What rivalry to be the first to grab the metal handle and force it up and down until the water spurted in bursts from it's mouth like opening. What joyous fun to some can be an arduous task for others. I'm certain that the cottars or farm workers families, occupants of the nearby cottages found the carrying distance, of their domestic water supply no laughing matter.

Onward and forward towards Taranty Village, (Trinity always sounds very 'bool in the mooth' to a Brechiner). Along past the golf course and the 'killing house', facing the beauties of Wirren, and White and Brown Caterthuns. The historical interests of Brown Caterthun and it's primitive secrets almost as old as time itself. Through Little Brechin, past Cookston then the welcome relief to pause and view the wonders of Chief Constable Bruce's garden. Snow white and the seven dwarfs, a windmill with a pond in front which appeared to have bubbling water and a resident duck, little paths through colourful floral displays with ornaments in secluded niches. Down past the 'Doctors Dam' and across the road at the Northport Distillery.

On good days if we had the energy left, we were allowed to visit Mrs Moyes's shoppie. (Better known later as Abbies). If you chose something from the many sweetie jars and it was on one of the higher up shelves, you were told 'That's a queer thing to ask for, pick something from lower down.' I still don't like Brandy Balls, from the easily reached shelf.

The Denside was busy with people tending their plots. Fresh vegetables were produced in abundance, many women becoming expert gardeners. If Granny was on duty after the Sunday school it was always the same walk. 'Round the Cemetery'. A very popular pastime by many locals. What a wealth of information recorded on those stone memorials. My imagination was fired by one particular epitaph of a poor soul 'cruelly murdered by the Mexicans'. Granny would get sat down in the little housie in the then New Section, with her friend to exchange news and gossip and more than likely have a puff at an illicit Woodbine. Meantime we were allowed freedom to wander at will.

I can remember when all the unused ground of the cemetery was utilised for growing carrots in the Dig for Victory Campaign. I still can spend many pleasurable hours in cemeteries and graveyards reading details from stones. My obsession for family history research was perhaps prompted by Grannie's Sunday afternoon walks, when I was young.

6

Brechin Rail

Coming down the Arbroath Road the other Sunday morning we were privileged to watch a steam train majestically rolling forward into the area of Brechin Station, the carriages gleaming in the bright sunlight under a halo of white smoke. What stories could be told about events and happenings involving what was once the centre of transport of goods and passengers embarking and disembarking from our Ancient City.

In my young days the rail company ran a regular service to Montrose, Forfar and Edzell. Things were rather different then in so many ways. There were many industries to be supplied with raw materials and their finished products conveyed to their ultimate destinations. Dukes and Smarts linen manufacturers, Coventry Gauge & Tool Co, Tecalamit making parts to aid the War effort, Black's sawmills and also all the food supplies and goods for retail outlets. The transporting of the Royal Mail to and from the Brechin district was another duty of the branch line staff. Fuel for motorised transport was not available without special permits. Public transport was the main means of travel. No flights to Disneyland or Spanish beaches for us. Instead it was Chivers berryfields, then after the fruit was all safely gathered in you could look forward to your reward for four weeks hard work.

What a treat to get your annual holiday - a day trip on the train to Montrose. It was all bustle at the station, with its newspaper kiosk and chocolate machines. There was no chocolate though because there was a war on. No corridor trains either - it was individual compartments to seat eight adults, with doors opening directly on to the platform. The carriage doors had windows which were lowered on large leather straps to allow access to the handle on the outside of the door.

"Keep back from there now, you might fall out onto the line," we were warned. After much rivalry and bickering as to who would sit in the four window seats, excitement was at fever pitch. Would the locomotive never move us out past the 'manurie' (Brechin Agricultural Trading Company) on the left and the coal yards on the right, then under the bridge beside the cattle market? By the time we had reached this stage we had been chastised several times for pulling down the window blinds, had already moved the heating control above the seat numerous times, felt the pipes below the seats for any change in temperature, been refused anything to eat from the picnic in brown paper carrier bags stored on the net luggage rack overhead, examined and read the message beside the communication cord to stop the train in an emergency.

"Come down from there and don't touch that chain or we will end up in the jail."

The journey was quite an undertaking for parents with small children. Being a branch line via Bridge of Dun and Dubton stations, it was necessary to change trains before reaching Montrose.

Up a narrow close, beside Woolies, then down by the Auld Kirk, past Paton's Mill, then on towards the beach. Anti tank barriers and barbed wire did not spoil our fun splashing in the waves or burying ourselves in the sand. A picnic with tea from a real Thermos Flask, bought with the necessary authorisation permit, was so grand. On the way back to the station we were given a pokie of chips and a small bottle of lemonade with a straw. This was really living the good life.

By the time we arrived back near Brechin we were looking out for all the things familiar to us. Black's woodyard, the Electric works, the Goods yard and the Petrol depot. Only part of a day away and we were so anxious to see our own familiar station again. How many weary travellers longed to see those sights before us.

Brechin's finest men had left from there to fight in The Great War, some never to return. World War II had caused a similar exodus. Of course the feeling of the great unknown awaited many who disembarked onto the platforms. Train loads of evacuees, moved to the safety of Angus homes from the devastation and death, caused by the bombing of their home towns by the German airforce. The Hospital trains bringing wounded soldiers from the front lines for treatment at the newly built military hospital at Stracathro. All the able bodied were recruited as stretcher bearers to assist in the transfer of the wounded tommies.

My experience at the station was dramatic but less patriotic. The evening papers arrived by train. My friend delivered for Eatons, the newsagent, near the Southport. All the paper laddies and lasses would hang about on the platform waiting for the paper train. I had no paper round but joined my friend with the others in the game with the porters barrows. The game got a bit rowdy resulting in the barrow falling off the platform onto the line. The porter, I think his name was Souter, left no doubt as to his opinion of our behaviour. I never waited for the paper train again, but I did sometimes take a short cut from the Squarie through the coalyards to the Bog Road.

Muir & Patton, Smith & Hood and the Co-operative - all different merchants, with their workmen filling coals from wagons into bags, weighing them before stacking on horse drawn flatcarts to deliver to their various domestic and industrial customers. At the goods yard in Bog Road, Wordies horse drawn carriers delivered most of the merchandise for local destinations.

Yes it was a busy place the Station, but like so many others and not all of them men, I find fascination in the power of a steam engine and a journey by rail. Someday soon I promise myself to leave Brechin by rail and enjoy all the pleasure memories bring of days when I was young, of a steam train journey to Bridge of Dun.

7

Health

I'm sure Gregor Fisher in his Rab C Nesbitt television series has often hit a note that says 'I remember that'. The other night his actions stirred up a series of memories that set me going. How well I remember those days when I was young, when Sunday nights meant down on bended knees. No it wasn't what Sunday's are meant for kneeling in prayer, but down with head bowed in front of mother, armed with a small tooth comb. The very thought of it makes my scalp feel tender.

"Has the beastie wife not been at the school for a while?" was a common question. After almost half an hour of scraping and searching over a folded newspaper you were granted the privilege of a shampoo with Derbac Soap, guaranteed to kill off all lice and nits. The district nurse, who did all sorts of duties from midwife to big game hunting for lice had not had time to visit Damacre School in the past week.

"Any spots or rashes?" was her usual question as she ruffled up the hair on the back of your neck. Sister MacFarlane, of the Queens District Nursing Service, must be fondly remembered by many Brechiners, some of whom she brought into this World. Health care responsibilities were undertaken in association with the General Practitioners, Doctors Dempster, Anderson and Lang. No grand health centre for them. Consultations were taken in a designated room within their own homes. Doctor Dempster lived in the house known as Westwood, in Castle Street where a complex for the elderly now stands. After he returned to China as a medical missionary the patients he tended were looked after either by Doctor Lang in Church Street or Doctor Anderson in Pearse Street. A visit to one of those surgeries or a call out for a home visit should have cost money as the National Health

Service with free medical care for all was a post War dream.

You could always tell the people who suffered from Impetigo a condition linked with lice infestation, for they were painted blue. Not as the early inhabitants of Brechin, the Picts, who painted their bodies blue, but with the new miracle cure for all - Gentian Violet.

Then there were those who suffered from Scabies or the 'Itch' a parasitic condition which was highly contagious. During the War mothers were very health and hygiene conscious. Friday nights you were given a liberal dose of Syrup of Figs or Castor Oil, 'just to clear out your system'. Saturday mornings before joining the food queues was spent in the outside lavatory expelling all that made your blood impure. It was considered a definite must to have a child's tonsils and adenoids removed to avoid the risk of illness and infection.

How well I remember this encounter as a hospital patient. I was taken up to the Infirmary one morning at nine o'clock by my mother, who had instructed me, if I behaved myself then I would get a surprise parcel. I still remember trying to focus on the pages of a book as my mother left me in the ward, but the tears won the battle.

Molly Mitchell (later to become the wife of Gordon Morrison) was in the bed next to me. "Look how Molly is behaving, she's not a cry baby" was told to me. Oh how often in later life I wished I had such stamina. The emotional upset and screaming got me first on the list to have my tonsils and adenoids removed. That must have been a short reign of peace and quiet while I was under anaesthetic for before mid day Miss McKenzie, the Infirmary matron contacted my mother to take me home.

With the War on there was neither ambulance or taxi available. I was taken home in my younger brothers pram. I've often wondered how long Molly Mitchell, was hospitalised because of her good behaviour?

Despite the Syrup of Figs treatment and the regular daily intake of Cod Liver Oil and Extract of Malt as so many others at the time, I did fall victim to an epidemic of Scarlet Fever. The fever ambulance from Forfar was sent for to take me and my younger brother to Whitehills Hospital at Forfar.

The Brechin Fever Hospital, a brick built building, between the Infirmary and the Cemetery had long been out of use. The vehicle was quite distinctive with its bell on front and a uniformed nurse in the passenger seat. Once admitted into the ward you were only allowed to communicate with any visitors, through the closed window.

My brother, as was the practice, had his hair shaved off, to alleviate the fever. I can remember my mother's astonishment when finally accepting the shorn pathetic figure was her son. No hugs or cuddles allowed, only faces through glass. In our three weeks confinement, and absence from home, everything had been fumigated and disinfected.

On discharge I was taken by my mother to the bus stop at Forfar High Street, for the journey home. My brother was detained for a further length of time, as he contracted chickenpox in a cross infection. How many remember the fever hospital? - fortunately we have progressed with preventive healthcare.

With a war on our mothers did their best to make certain we were well looked after. A good scrub standing in the wash boiler, in an outside wash house after washing day, could equal any session in a jacuzzi. With cleanliness next to Godliness did we achieve anything from our Sunday evenings on bended knees. More than likely a few prayers were said, for the combing session to come to an end.

Treatment at a hospital outwith your own residential area with separation from those nearest and dearest. Living has become so sophisticated and advanced during my lifetime but have we moved in the right direction away from the amenities and things on offer in Brechin in days even before I was young?

8

Go up the Street

G o up the Street and get it", a simple enough phrase. What street you might ask? Any Brechiner would immediately know what was meant by the phrase. A shopping expedition to the shops located in the High Street. How well I knew these establishments in the days when I was young. Supermarkets with their queues at checkouts were nonexistent then. The queues weren't though, for with a war on, food and clothing were rationed to ensure that everyone was entitled to a fair share. The queues were a good indication that a shop had something out of the ordinary for sale. Powdered eggs or perhaps fresh fruit which could only be purchased by someone holding a child's green ration card. Strange to recall how even bread and potatoes were exchanged for coupons.

Saturday mornings it was my duty to shop for my great aunt who did not finish work at 'Dukies' until one o'clock. That was the half day, after five days of working from six in the morning to six at night. I was under strict instruction to buy various items from selected shops. Bile Beans and Union Jack corn paste from Crockett the chemist. What a wonderful shop, with its various coloured jars and bottles. On the counter was a gas jet with a naked flame. Should you require medication Mr Crockett would wrap the bottle in an expertly folded paper then close it with a blob of sealing wax, melted at the flame.

There were so many home remedies to be had before consulting the doctor, who would require to be paid for a consultation. Blanchards Pink Pills, for pale people, a cure for adults needing a pick me up. Children were given Farish's chemical food as a tonic. Ipecacuanha and Syrup of Squills mixture, a bitter tasting remedy that would speed up any recovery to stop having to swallow it.

A visit to Alex Low the butcher, on the other side of Gellatly's bakehouse close, from the Misses Whitlaw's china shop, and next to Mitchell's the jewellers. "Lovely cut of corned beef here, straight from the tin," he was quite a joker. Butter and cheese from the 'Maypole' further up the street next to Carmichaels shoe shop.

Once before going back to school after the summer holidays, auntie had taken me up the close to make certain I had no holes in my socks, before buying me shoes in Carmichaels. What a wonderful machine they had, it showed an X Ray type image of your foot inside the shoe. Across the street was Callander's gents outfitters. Each side of the shop doorway was a full length mirror. It was said "If you look in the mirrors you can see Callander's monkey." It took me years to work that one out.

Back down to the Cross to a little tobacconists, Strattons, for an ounce of 'Taddy' snuff. I believe it was a common practice among weavers and those who worked in Dukie's and Smartie's to clear their heads of the dust and stour by snuffing. Smoking tobacco in or near the weaving sheds was strictly forbidden because of the fire risk associated with workers having 'a fly puff'.

Down to Webster's the newsagent for 'The Picture Post', 'Everybody's' and 'The Peoples Friend'. With very few houses with electric power, no television and wireless requiring the regular charging of the wet accumulators linked with power from a high tension battery, reading was a favourite past time. Websters, as did other newsagents, ran a private book lending service, for a small fee.

Sometimes I did get things wrong like the time I was told to get a sponge. I thought I was so grand handing over three pounds in Stenhouse the chemist for what must have been the only natural sponge in Brechin, with the War being on. "It was a baked sponge from Belford's bakery in Market Street you should have got. Take that back and get the money for it."

It was a very meek and mild me who said "It's not what auntie wanted. Can I have her money back please." Three pounds was more than the week's wages for those long hours she had worked.

There were goods to be bought at the doors of peoples homes. The Arbroath fish wives came certain days, on Nelson's bus, and sold fish from creels strapped to their backs. They were most distinctive in their uniform type dress. Vegetables, grown in his market garden at Banks of Brechin, were sold from a horse drawn cart by Mr Duncan, Denburn Bakery sold pies, buns and cakes from a covered handcart. The trays of goods must have been very heavy to push up the hills and braes of Brechin. Anne MacGregor could be depended upon to always be at her designated sales pitch, on time, come hail, rain or shine.

After work with the bakers Anne took on her important role of 'Young Peoples Sergeant Major' with the Salvation Army. So many of my age group will remember the hours of work and patience Anne put into her duties. During her lunch break Anne's barrow could be found parked in the wide pend beside the Salvation Army headquarters in Union Street. No security locks, burglar alarms or surveillance cameras to protect the goods. The barrow was quite safe as people passed to 'Go up the Street' in my young day.

9

River

The sight of the River Southesk flowing under the Brechin Bridge means so many different things to so many people, of the past and present. There must be many who have memories of a childhood playing on its bonny banks, those who have worked in the mills and factories initially sited by its side for the power the water supplied to drive machinery.

How well I can recall the stories told to me about the East Mill, a spinning works driven by water, fed by a lade from the river just opposite the laundry. Part of the mill can still be seen today but it's now dilapidated state shrouds such an important part of local history. The silent bell tower no longer summons workers to tend the frames used to produce thread for the weavers. Most of the spinners attended the half time school in Union Street, either mornings or afternoons according to the shift they were required to work. It wasn't all work and no play, by what Granny said, for there was time to play hopping games on the flagged passes between the frames. They all had to run for their lives when the mill caught fire and the bell sounded the alarm. All before my young days.

I do recall all the paper mill buildings in the Inch. Production had long since stopped but they were used as a store for waste paper collected for recycling, during the War. I do remember the flooding of River street when each year it was a common ritual to sand bag all the doorways and close entrances from the Bridge-end Bar to the Faird Moo. The bottom of the Vennel was always worst affected, but despite this offers of rehousing to higher and drier accommodation were annually refused. It was considered a privilege to reside in River Street and Bridge Street.

Only those of my age group and older will easily recall the area covered by the flood water. That mysterious hold of the river and all it entails in associated memories can always link Brechiners together. What fun to run home from school, on the light nights and run down the mill stairs, past Dakers weaving sheds, back gate of the castle, along to the high railings at the start of the Inch. There we would climb over those six foot high spikes to get access to The Islandies. Oh what fun and delight to scramble across the rocks with the castle high above us in an air of overall protectiveness. It did not stop me from picking up a rusted fishing hook in my toe and having to confess I'd been to a forbidden playground. "There have been people drowned in that river," was a true but unheeded warning. How many Brechiners learned to swim at the Paperie or Lido?

A Sunday afternoon pastime for the young adults was to hire one of Haggart's boats and row down river as far as the Bridge. On this great adventure they would probably pass people feeding ducks and swans or fishermen casting flies to lure a fresh run salmon. Another favourite of the young men was to try their skills at Haggarts target shooting range. The Inch was the place where the circus set up their Big Top. The Paperie was looked over by the new flats built at the Meikle Mill. Affectionately known to Brechiners as Pee View.

This was recently brought to mind when I was showing my grandchildren the house I was born in. "Granny was born in a house with a sign for a toilet," they laughed. Further down river, past the East Mill, later to become the Tecalamit, across a large pipe then onwards to the wonders of the Dennies. What theme park could offer the pleasures we had playing on the middle bank, between the Southesk and the lade. A rope swing from a tree which if you ran down the banking could launch you right into the middle of the river. Of course on odd occasions your hands, burned by the rope, let go and down you went with a splash. Another explanation conjured up for returning home.

All types of imaginary situations were acted out in the bushes. Depending on which film had featured most recently at the matinee. Cowboys and Indians with tepees and cabins formed of fallen branches. Wild berries, rose hips, beech nuts all eagerly searched for and devoured. Whistles made from fresh green bark of the trees. Water pistols made from the stalks of 'scabbie flourish'. Wild flowers in abundance and competition was keen to find as many different varieties as possible. This was a far cheaper game than collecting scraps of angels, as you could present the teacher at school next day with a lovely bouquet, picked only for her.

The middle bank ended at Craig Pool, where the salmon would lie in abundance before their long journey back to their spawning ground. This was where the lade and the river rejoined, well into the Kinnaird estate. This was an area taboo to us for swimming and perhaps we honoured this ruling because of the knowledge that the nearby sewage works discharged effluent into the river nearby.

The river between the Islandies and the Stannochy was relatively unknown to us as this was within the castle policies. On days when the castle grounds were open for charitable occasions it was possible to see the private or Image bridge across the Southesk. Alas the East Mill, Tecalamit, Smarties, Dukies, Papermill and Backie braes are no longer with us. Gone are the rowing boats on the river like so many other things supposed to be progress towards a better way of living.

Will the Brechiners of today when my age remember so many happy hours and pleasure spent by the river, when I was young? Only the water rushing from the hills towards the sea, as it has done since time began will know the answer to that question.

10

Recycling

Everywhere you can find them. Collection skips for clear glass, grccn glass, cotton goods, woollen, clothes for reuse.

It would seem that we have all of a sudden become a nation aware of the need to slow down the amount of waste our country generates every single day. This recycling project is by no means a brain wave of today's bright boffins. People born before the second World War, of my age group and older, will distinctly recall how little waste there was to be found at the end of each day, from the average family home.

In the first instance there was a short supply of money, which in itself promoted careful use of all material things. The sound of a bugle in the street heralded the arrival of the ragman's horse and cart on a collection round.

"Bring out your woollen rags and get the bairns a gold fish." I desperately wanted one of those fish for a pet. "You must have something old and woollen Granny," I nagged at her. I can picture it yet as she pulled off her working cardigan. "Take the clothes off my back and maybe I'll get a minutes peace." I got the fish in a jam jar - a fair exchange for Granny's jumper that was darned, patched and most probably handed on by several owners before her. Needless to say that the fish had not survived very long.

The jam jar would have been stored and along with others exchanged at Raggie Murray's in City Road for cash. In some towns it was an accepted practice that two jam jars paid entrance to the cinema. Glass lemonade bottles were another good source of pocket money if collected and returned to the shops. Even the ones that had been stored under the bed for days in the production of that fabulous drink, Sugarelly Water, made from a stick of hard liquorice shaken vigorously, then stored in the dark.

With a War on and everything rationed and produced under the utility regulations, new clothes were something of a novelty. Outgrown or part worn garments were handed from family to family depending on who had someone the size and shape to fit. Fashion never seemed to be part of the equation.

"Run up to the meal store, in Swan Street, or Gellatly's bake house and see if they've any old flour bags." Washed and bleached they could be turned into pillowcases, tablecloths, blouses, knickers - in fact anything Granny set her mind on having.

When wearing apparel could no longer be considered respectable enough to be seen in public then it was handed over to Grandad. On the dark winter nights he spent many hours with a home made cleek looping multi coloured strips of rags through a canvas bag, ultimately ending up with a brightly designed and patterned hearth rug. Blankets thin with many years of service were revitalised when covered with squares of material from all types of items. Flannel shirts, curtains, aprons, dresses anything at all. It was a good game to play at night looking at the various patches and remembering where you had last seen them.

Jumble sales at the Sallies were a great source of materials for re-fashioning. A man's large woollen pullover could be 'rattled down' the wool washed and then knitted into several smaller garments. "Hold your arms up and still," what a tiresome job it was, holding up the hanks of wool until they could be wound into a ball. "There you've let some drop and it's all tangled up now." The agony prolonged until the knots were unravelled.

The final parting with woollens and clothes was normally at the time of the Spring cleaning. "Take those bags of rags to the store and see what you can get for them." The rag store was later to become the property of Brechin Silver band.

"Clean woollens over there and others to this side," was Mrs Murray's instructions. After weighing the separate lots you were given a cash settlement for the unwanteds. Rabbit skins were much sought after, with regular door to door calls requesting the honour of 'taking them off your hands'. Food including meat being rationed and living in a rural area they must have done a good business, as many a Sunday dinner started off in a poachers pocket. Any household garbage such as vegetable peelings were quickly added to the compost heap or collected in bins as swill for the local pig farmers. Aggie Cross, who had a shop in Union Street, kept a pig in her garden.

The age of plastic containers had still not arrived which meant that most packaging was of paper or cardboard. Apart from what was utilised for cutting into squares for delicate personal use, all newspapers, wrappings and clean paper was carefully stored and collected by the 'scaffies' on refuse day. Old prams, bicycles and bits of toys were turned into carties or saved as spares. Broken or unwanted furniture was used to fuel the fires for heating when coals were in short supply. Zinc buckets, some still with the obvious white and maroon paint from the berryfields were filled with ashes from the open fires in every home and set out for collection on the day appointed by the Brechin Cleansing department. There never appeared to be any other types of rubbish left on the pavements.

Certainly nothing to put in today's selection of multi-coloured wheelie bins. With the advent of smoke free zones and central heating then surely it should mean a reduction in the amount of garbage needing uplifted. No ashes for a start.

Recycling collection points overflowing and yet we need the emptying service of the blue, black, brown and green chest high receptacles at least weekly or at regular intervals. Can we lay the blame at the invention of our age, the essential plastic material.

There certainly wasn't all that rubbish when I was young.

11

Food

There is not a day, or evening that passes without the television presenting to the media, numerous cookery programmes. The wonderful exotic dishes that can be produced by experienced masters of the kitchen, leave viewers with mouths watering, or twisted up at the idea of swallowing delicacies alien to our taste. With that in mind I have often thought what Granny would have said about the foods we eat as part of our daily intake. Indian and Chinese take-aways, Deep fried Mars bars with chips, pizzas of every description, fried seaweed.

Now perhaps she would have agreed to sample the last one as it was not so far removed from one of her little treats. Dulse roasted with a red hot poker. This form of sea plant would have been gathered at the same time as a large pot full of buckies, when the family had a day trip to Buddon Ness. After being cleaned and boiled the contents of the shells hooked out from their hiding place on the end of a pin. You could taste the sea. Perhaps age and years of chewing dulls the taste buds, as nothing ever seems to be as mouth watering fresh as when you were young.

Taranty tomatoes are still excellent but nothing to match those of bygone years, collected straight from the hot houses. Maybe the run out to collect them and the return run added to the flavour. Perhaps it was Granny's tip of always dipping them in sugar to 'kill the acid', that made them perfect.

Yoghurts and Fromage Fraise were unheard of, but again we did enjoy a similar dish. "Take the jug and run across to Christie's dairy and get two pints from the milking." The dairy was behind Viewforth Terrace a large tenement building facing the older built houses in Hillview. After numerous little mouthfuls from the rim of the jug, 'just to keep it from spilling over' the contents were safely delivered into Granny's hands. Warm fresh milk has a taste that cannot be compared with any other. The jug was emptied into a large bowl, flavouring and essence of rennet added. Given time to settle and we had delicious curds and whey.

Beside the dairy was a small market garden worked by Mr Pirie. The vegetables were picked straight from the earth and carried back to Granny's in an old enamel basin. "Now while I'm washing and cutting up these, you run along to the butchery at Andra Cross's Soshie and get a 'bit tae boil' for the soup pot." It was not until adulthood that I discovered there was no such cut of meat named 'tae boil'.

Another favourite request was to get several 'mealie jerkers'. That's one bit of information that has passed down the generations as my grandson recognises them as his most favourite food. To those uninitiated they are white puddings, excellent on their own or served with mince and tatties. Granny's soup always had large pieces of tattie and neep which were saved on the plate after supping the broth. Mashed up together with a fork, then sprinkled with oatmeal, what a grand accompaniment they made to the slices of boiled beef.

Oatmeal played a big part in the diet when I was young. I can remember when Grandad came home from Dukies at breakfast time his porridge was ready on the table, served up in a bowl, with the cream of the milk served in a smaller side bowl. Grandad spooned the porridge through the cream before swallowing. Certainly it tastes different, but then it was not quick boil oats or Readybrek, oatmeal soaked overnight, then boiled for an hour to smooth out any lumps. Well worth the bother. Oatmeal soaked in water also made a grand refreshing drink in hot weather. There was no waste as any not consumed could be used as a beauty aid for a facial treatment.

A great mealtime favourite was hot cooked tripe. This was sold by several shops, as was hough. Scott's, in Montrose

Street, sold a variety of cooked meats. I believe it is now a shoe shop. "Take a jug and run to the Soshie butcher at the top of the Den and get some tripe." The look of it was enough for me, like strips of towelling. I was later to discover that there were two varieties the other being honeycomb. This was similar to parts of stewed bathing caps. When the order was for hot hough, I managed numerous sips from the delicious smelling liquid, just to avoid spillage.

The other smell that brings a moistness to my mouth was the smell of new baked bread. "Get away to Gellatly's in Montrose Street." For some reason I was always told to get a plain 'cutting' loaf. That was one which was a day older and easy to cut with a knife, probably making it more economical. How often I said there was no old bread left in order to get a freshly made warm loaf. I would then have to hand over the tissue paper, wrapped around two crusts with the middle picked away and eaten on the journey along the street. I always thought it was only the well off people who bought pan loafs.

With the wartime shortages there was always corned beef for the weekly allowance. Served with stovies and oatcakes I'm certain it would make any of today's cordon bleu chefs sit up and take notice. Herring bought by the basin full from a 'cadger' from Montrose, who sometimes arrived in Brechin with a horse and cart. The fish were cleaned and coated with egg and oatmeal then baked slowly in the oven until golden brown. Absolutely delicious. Despite rationing and food restrictions we never went hungry. The oatmeal most probably came from the mill at Balbirnie, or perhaps sold by some farm worker who as part of their wages or arrals, were given an allowance of several stones of oatmeal each working term. A term being the length of a fee, from twenty eighth of May to the twenty eighth of November.

The feeing markets were sometimes held at the Cross, but that like other things is now past history, as are many of the happenings of when I was young.

12

Entertainment

The end of summer and the drawing in of the nights turns thoughts to indoor leisure pursuits and hobbies. "What did you do on the dark evenings when you were young Granny?" gave me reason to think back more years than I would like to admit. For a start there were no televisions, computers and the many electronic games our children take for granted.

There of course is the advantage of them being masters of the mouse and screen. I still feel embarrassed at having to request the assistance of our grandchildren to set the timer on the video recorder. After an hour lying on my stomach, several changes of glasses to peer at the flashing numbers, I admit defeat, and hand over to those of superior knowledge.

However, I could still manage to entertain myself and others should there for some reason be a power cut off to the modern day wonder machines. Family parties were the occasions when everyone performed their own piece. Grandad's rendering of 'Who killed Cock Robin?', brought a tear to many an eye. It was not the pathetic story of the bird's fate that caused the frequent wiping of eyes, but Grandad's solemn bellowing out of verse after verse causing the stifling of laughter and giggles. Then there was uncle Jim, minus his false teeth, dressed in Granny's flannelette nightdress, with the tea cosy on his head, telling the story of Mad Karoo and the Green Eye of the Little Yellow God.

Of course the scene was livened up at such get togethers as wedding celebrations. A musician was engaged to assist with the evenings jollifications. The most popular being Harry the Fiddler. Harry Sim, was a very talented and accomplished musician. I believe he left his English home to take up an appointment in Brechin, playing the musical accompaniment to the silent picture shows. No special sound equipment and amplifiers, in fact I cannot recall seeing Harry with sheet music, but he could match any of today's top violinists.

Receptions were normally in the evenings as there was no one who could afford to have time off work. Most of the guests would be wearing their service uniforms as with the War on clothing was rationed. Thinking of musicians who were outstanding in my young mind, evenings spent at the Salvation Army were joyous occasions, listening to expertly played instruments. Apart from the Harmonium and Brass section I can vividly recall Anne McGregor playing the concertina to accompany Miss Smith on the 'mouthie'. This expert of the 'sook and blaw' was in height around four feet eleven inches and the Harmonica she mastered was about one foot in length. As an encore she would play her other mouthie, which was about one inch long and held between her lips. All before Larry Adler became famous.

Of course as Young Soldiers we were all trained in the expertise of tambourine playing. There were many such as myself With Joy in their Hearts and Cups Full and Running Over. The Army Citadel of today was then the meeting place of the Town Mission. John Oswald, of the Damacre Road Smiddy and bicycle shop, was the man in charge. Magic lantern shows depicting the Mission's work in foreign fields was meant to inspire in us a feeling for those under privileged, however, as all other children we became bored.

Noting that the slide was changed when the speaker stamped his foot, soon the whole meeting place was resounding to the sound similar to a marching army. There were the nights when we did 'our duty to honour the King and help others at all times, and obey the Brownie Law'. This was alright in the summer time as the Brownie Pack met at the old curling pond, now Mountskip. Brown Owl's name was Knowles and either she or her family kept goats. This fact is imprinted on my unmentionable as a horned and bearded one ran head first into my sitting down part and tore my uniform. I think that was the end of my helping others at all times and obeying the Brownie Law.

I did enjoy the walk back on the light nights especially the pokie of chips from Granties, The Savoy, in Market Street. With the black out and no street lights it would have been impossible to attend in winter. Perhaps this was the real reason for my being lapsed.

There were internationally famous stars who performed for Brechin audiences. The Workers Playtime radio series was recorded at least once that I can remember from the canteen of the Coventry Tool & Gauge company. No Matrix in these times. Workers came by bus from Forfar, Dundee, Montrose and Arbroath to help keep up the twenty four hours production line. Entertainment during one meal break was provided by none other than that grand Lancashire lass, star of stage, screen and radio, Gracie Fields and her husband Monty Banks.

I can hear the young ones, "You've never really answered our question, what did you do?" I suppose as every one else of my era, I joined in with whatever was going on. Certainly I cannot remember us ever getting into bother and standing around moaning about boredom and nowhere to go.

There is of course the other aspect maybe - in true entertainment style of the ceilidh I am nothing more than a Seanachaidh, or teller of tales.

For The Brechiner